CONTENT

SECTION

I THE PROBATE PROCESS

When someone dies, their affairs are sorted out by people known as their personal representatives. If there is a valid will, this will normally name one or more executors to act as personal representatives. If there is no will, close relatives apply to the Court to be appointed as administrators, with a similar role.

The first task of the personal representatives is to establish that they have the legal authority to do the job (so that organisations holding the deceased's money, for example, are able to release it). For executors, this is called **seeking probate**; administrators apply for **letters of administration**. In either case, an office of the High Court known as the Probate Registry is the body that can give the authority – it has 30 main offices across the country, with local offices open for restricted hours in 90 smaller towns.

Once probate or letters of administration have been granted, the personal representatives move on to the administration of the estate (what the deceased has left). If there is a valid will, this normally means carrying out the instructions contained within it. If not, the estate is wound up in accordance with the legal rules of intestacy (see box on p4).

This Pack takes you step by step through the administration of an estate, from seeking probate (or letters of administration) to the final winding-up. It explains in plain English what you must do and gives examples of letters and calculations. It includes checklists to help you do the job properly. And it explains how to fill in the official forms.

In some cases, professional help is needed to complete the job – see opposite. But this is an area of the law where the lay person is positively encouraged to get involved: there is a personal application department in each Probate Registry designed to assist the amateur. Most people should be able to tackle the task of seeking probate without difficulty unless there are the sort of complications listed opposite.

WHAT IS INVOLVED

The main tasks of the personal representatives are as follows:

- find out what the deceased has left, and also what debts have to be repaid
- work out approximately how much inheritance tax will be due and raise the cash to pay it
- complete the forms required by the Probate Registry – including the inheritance tax return for the Inland Revenue
- visit the Probate Registry in person to swear the papers
- pay the inheritance tax
- receive the grant of probate or letters of administration
- use the grant to get hold of the assets in the estate
- sell any property if necessary
- pay any debts
- hand over any legacies and bequests
- deal with whatever is left (the **residue** – normally divided between one or more beneficiaries).

Flowchart A in the back pocket of this Pack sets out all the tasks which must be done. Checklist B, also in the back pocket, provides a detailed list of the steps, which you can use as a master plan to keep track of progress.

PROFESSIONAL HELP

If you decide after looking through the contents of this Pack that you'd rather not devote the time and effort to dealing with probate, you can hand the task over to a professional adviser. You will also find that Flowchart A in the back pocket directs you towards professional advice in certain circumstances.

If you go to a professional adviser, there will be fees to pay which you can pay from the estate. A solicitor will normally charge a lump sum which reflects the amount of work involved, plus a percentage of the value of the estate (commonly 1½%). High Street bank executor departments generally cost somewhat more. Ask for an estimate before making a decision.

There are some circumstances in which it is essential to get professional help. For example, if the deceased:

- owned a business or farm (or was personally engaged in any other business activity)
- was involved in family trusts
- has made substantial bequests to children under 18
- left a badly drawn-up home-made will
- appears not to have provided for someone who partly or wholly depended on him/her (or made inadequate provision): such dependants may be able to claim reasonable provision from the estate under the Inheritance (Provision for Family and Dependants) Act 1975
- died intestate leaving a spouse – the distribution of the estate may involve the complication of a 'lifc interest' (see Box on intestacy overleaf)
- owned considerable assets outside the UK
- died intestate leaving a relative who is entitled to a share of the estate but who has vanished (again, see Box on intestacy overleaf).

WHEN PROBATE IS NOT NEEDED

In some cases, there is no need to seek probate or letters of administration:

- if the estate is only cash (notes and coin) and personal effects (clothing, furniture and a car, for example); so long as there are no bank accounts, shares, pension arrears, house, etc the will's provisions can be carried out without formality (though where large amounts of cash are involved, seeking probate might prevent disputes later)
- if there is no more than £5,000 in total held in National Savings accounts, certain pension funds and friendly societies, whoever is entitled to the money simply writes to the organisation asking for the appropriate claim form which should be returned with a special £1.50 death certificate (see p6)
- if the deceased nominated investments to a particular person, these can be transferred to that person on production of a death certificate (the right to nominate certain National Savings investments and British Government stock was withdrawn in 1981, but nominations made before then stand unless the person who made it has married or revoked it, or the person nominated has died).

Intestacy

If there is no valid will, the deceased's estate is distributed according to the legal rules of intestacy. The rules for dealing with the deceased's property in England and Wales are illustrated in the diagram below.

Who your money would go to if you died without making a will (in England and Wales)

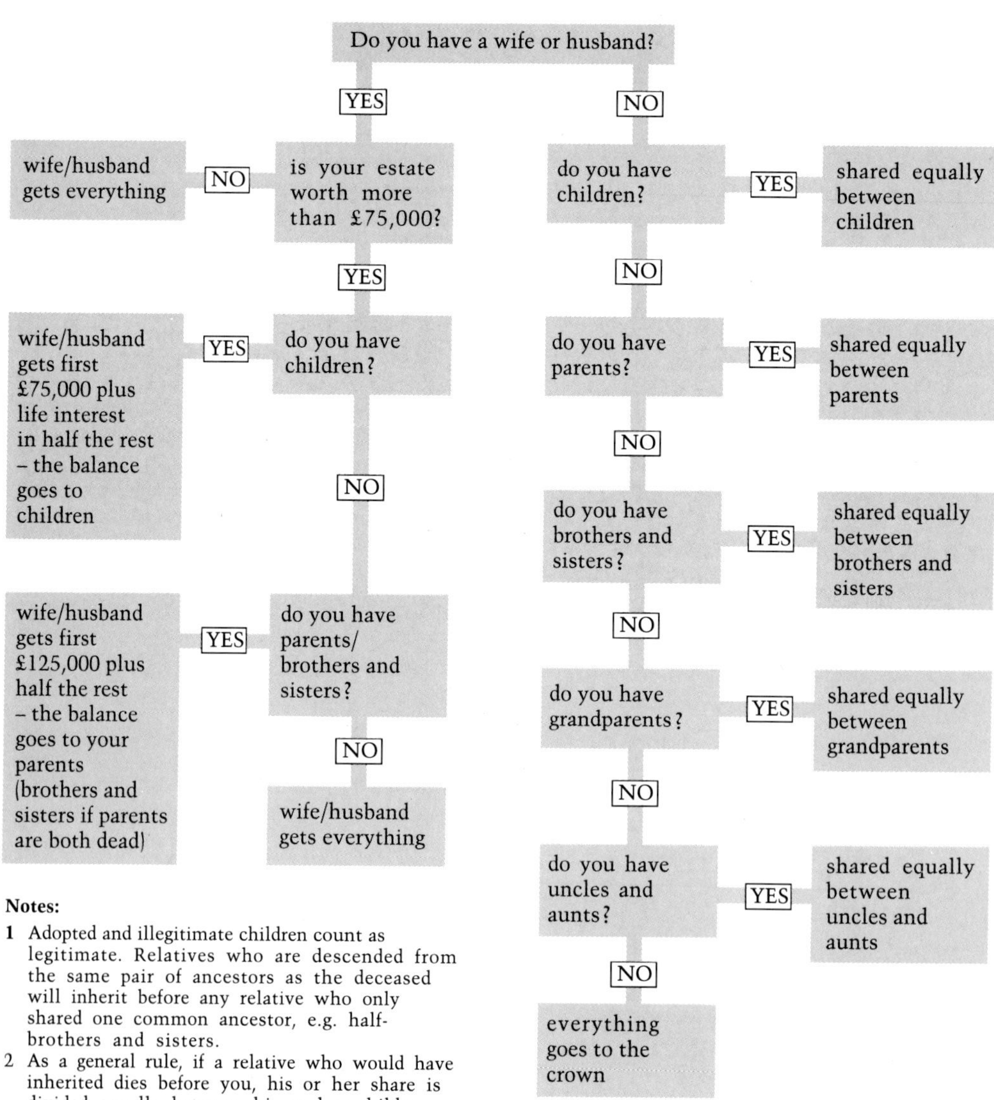

Notes:

1 Adopted and illegitimate children count as legitimate. Relatives who are descended from the same pair of ancestors as the deceased will inherit before any relative who only shared one common ancestor, e.g. half-brothers and sisters.

2 As a general rule, if a relative who would have inherited dies before you, his or her share is divided equally between his or her children, e.g. if you had a son and a daughter and the son predeceased you, his children – your grandchildren – would inherit his share.

3 The wife or husband always gets the personal effects, e.g. furniture, car – as well as any money they are entitled to.

4 If you share ownership of a house with your wife or husband (or anyone else) through a joint tenancy, your share automatically goes to the co-owner. With tenancy in common, your share of the house is distributed with the rest of your estate according to the rules above.

I

Intestacy, cont.

A valid will may still create a **partial intestacy**, if some of the deceased's property cannot be distributed under its terms. For example, if the residue is left to someone who has died and no alternative is specified in the will, the residue must be distributed according to the rules of intestacy (other valid bequests in the will can, however, be carried out in accordance with the deceased's wishes).

With a full intestacy, there will be no executors to act as personal representatives. Instead, the next-of-kin, in a fixed order of precedence, are entitled to apply for the grant of letters of administration. Applying for letters of administration is virtually identical to applying for probate.

The first person entitled to apply is the deceased's widow or widower. If there is no surviving spouse – or if he or she cannot act – then any of the children may apply. Grandchildren can also apply at this stage if their parents are dead.

Thereafter, the right to apply passes down the blood line of kinship:

- the deceased's parents
- brothers and sisters (or their children)
- half-brothers and -sisters (or their children)
- grandparents
- aunts or uncles (or their children)
- aunts or uncles of the half blood (or their children).

No other relative is entitled to apply. Nor are in-laws and people related by marriage. But illegitimate children may apply, as may adopted children.

The administrator's job follows much the same steps as the executor's. But instead of a will to follow, the net estate (after paying debts, funeral expenses, inheritance tax and expenses of administering the estate) is divided up according to the rules of intestacy.

SECTION

2 FIRST STEPS: GATHERING INFORMATION

The very first step in sorting out someone's will is to get hold of the will itself. For what to do if there is no will, see p4.

The will may be at the deceased's home – in which case all you need to do is search for it. A professionally drawn-up will is often stored at the office of the solicitor who drew it up. Or the will may be lodged at a bank.

Wills can also be lodged at Somerset House for a small charge: a deposit certificate is issued which is used to reclaim it. If this does not turn up, contact The Record Keeper, Principal Registry – Family Division, Somerset House, Strand, London WC2R 1LP.

Note that a will lodged with a solicitor, bank or Somerset House is not necessarily the last word. It's worth searching the deceased's papers in case there's a later will or codicils amending the earlier one.

The will doesn't have to be read formally – indeed, beneficiaries don't have to learn of their good fortune until probate is granted. But major beneficiaries should normally be told of the will's contents, with a warning that it may take some time to sort everything out.

THE DEATH CERTIFICATE

The first formality after someone dies is to register the death with the local Registrar of Births, Marriages and Deaths (address in the phone book). You can find out more about the immediate steps following death from *What to Do When Someone Dies*, available price £7.95 from Consumers' Association, P.O. Box 44, Hertford SG14 1SH.

The certificate of registration is free, and is used to claim various social security benefits (e.g. widow's pension). You will also need copies of the death certificate to start the probate process. Certified copies of the entry of death on the register come in various types:

- a standard death certificate (£2 in England & Wales) – several extra copies of this will come in handy for getting details together for probate
- for a child, adopted child, stepchild or grandchild to claim on a life insurance policy for the death of a parent or grandparent, a special death certificate is needed (costing £1.50)
- if the deceased had savings or life insurance with a registered friendly society, you will need a certificate 'for the purposes of the Friendly Societies Acts' (£1.50)
- a certificate for 'certain other statutory purposes' (£1.50) can be used to claim state benefits if the standard certificate has been lost. It is also used to get hold of National Savings investments if probate is not required (see p3).

THE EXECUTORS

The will should name at least one executor, and no more than four. It may also name one or more substitutes if any of the first choices cannot or will not act. The first step, therefore, is to see who is willing to act.

An executor who does not want to do the job should sign a form of renunciation (available from Oyez Stationery – see p32). Alternatively, the person can sign the **power reserved letter** which the Probate Registry will send when the time comes to apply for probate.

If an executor renounces, any substitute named in the will then takes over. If no substitute is named, the remaining executor(s) prepared to act can go ahead. And if none of the named executors can do the job, the will must be carried out by administrators appointed by the Court. The first person to whom the Court will grant letters of administration (if he/she applies) is the sole beneficiary of the will, or the residuary legatee to whom everything is left after specific bequests.

As an alternative to renouncing, an executor can appoint someone else to act as attorney (this is particularly appropriate if the executor is out of the country, or ill). An attorney – who doesn't have to be a solicitor – acts as if named as an executor in the will. A form for appointing an attorney is available from Oyez Stationery (see p32).

The executors can agree to instruct a solicitor to act for them, or do all the work themselves. Executors can delegate day-to-day matters to one of their number (it's best to authorise this in writing), though all the executors must sign the official papers.

Being an executor need not be unduly onerous, but there are important legal responsibilities. Executors owe a duty of 'utmost good faith' to the deceased, to people who are owed money from the estate and to the beneficiaries of the will. They must try to get the most out of the estate, and be able to show that they have not syphoned any of it off for their own use. Creditors and beneficiaries can challenge the executors if they feel that there has been any malpractice – so executors need to keep clear and accurate records.

They should also keep the administration of the estate separate from their own personal affairs. They can claim necessary expenses from the estate, but should be sure to keep accounts and receipts.

COLLECTING TOGETHER THE DETAILS

The first task for personal representatives is to compile a list of what's in the estate.

A useful first step is to arrange for the deceased's post to be redirected to you as executor. The Post Office will do this for a year for £16. This could help you find out about bank accounts, share holdings, etc, where the documents have gone missing. There's a form to apply for redirection, available from post offices: complete and return this with a copy of the death certificate and a letter explaining that you are acting as a personal representative.

A second step is to get hold of any paperwork the deceased had about his/her wealth: National Savings Certificates, life insurance policies, bank books, building society statements, Premium Bonds, share certificates, a copy of the last Tax Return and so on. You might also find details of pension schemes, employers who owe pay, the ownership of the home and other useful information. In some cases, deeds, certificates and other essential papers may be held at the deceased's bank. Remember to ask when sending for details of accounts.

Use these to compile a list of possessions and any debts. You'll find three Checklists in the back pocket of this Pack to help you collect the information:

- Checklist C lists possessions, valuables and debts
- Checklist D brings together details of savings accounts of all kinds and miscellaneous investments
- Checklist E is for stocks, shares and unit trusts.

These Checklists also have spaces for entering the value of each item.

Note that one of your duties as personal representative is to safeguard the assets of the estate. Where a home is involved, write to the insurance company that insures the building and contents (there may be a different one for each) to put them in the picture and make sure that the home remains covered. The same applies for insurance of assets like a car, caravan or valuables.

The home

The value of a home for probate purposes is what you would have got if you had sold it on the day of the death (with no deduction for the costs involved, such as solicitor's and estate agent's fees). The simplest way to put a figure on this is to get an estate agent to value the home – usually this is free. You can even value the home yourself. This may be quite straightforward with, for example, a standard estate house.

Alternatively, you can pay a surveyor or valuer to value a home (this might cost £50–£100, depending on the value). But this is not essential – and would be a waste of money where the home was passing to a spouse. However you go about it, the valuation will be checked by the District Valuer, an Inland Revenue official with access to all home sale prices in the area.

With a jointly owned home, the value of the deceased's share is worked out according to the type of joint ownership:

- if held as **joint tenants**, the share of the first to die automatically passes to the survivor on death (irrespective of what the will says). The value of this share is half the total value
- if held as **tenants in common**, the share of the first to die is part of the estate, and the will can specify what happens to it (it doesn't have to go to the joint owner). The normal rule for valuing an equal share is that it is somewhat less than half the total value, because a buyer would not be prepared to pay half the market value when there is someone else living in the home. But with a married couple, the value of an equal share is simply half the total value (to stop married couples artificially reducing the value of their estate for tax purposes).

If there's a mortgage owing on the home, write to the lender for details of the exact amount outstanding at the date of the death, sending a copy of the death certificate as proof of death. The sample letter opposite shows you how you might do this.

Possessions

There is no need to prepare a complete list of furniture and effects (clothing, jewellery, car and other personal possessions). Itemise anything worth much over £100 and put a lump sum valuation on the rest.

Dear Sir

Re: Alison Marilyn Brown deceased

I am executor of the will of the late Alison Marilyn Brown, who died on 7 April 1989. My co-executor is her daughter Beatrice Eleanor Cartwright of 17 Thresher Road, Slagthorpe, Borset. I enclose Mrs Brown's death certificate. Please return this when you have noted it in your records.

Mrs Brown owned the following house on which there is an outstanding mortgage with your society: 33 Acacia Avenue, Slagthorpe, Borset - mortgage no. 77/192837465. Please let me know exactly how much capital was outstanding on the mortgage at the date of death, and also any interest due up to that date.

Yours faithfully

The general rule is that an item's value is what you could have sold it for on the day of death. For household goods, this means what they might fetch at auction as secondhand goods – usually a fraction of their replacement value.

Even with more valuable possessions, the probate value is usually less than their replacement value. This is because a dealer would pay much less to buy it than he would sell it for – the mark-up can be half or more of the retail price. A jeweller will value jewellery for a fee which can be paid out of the estate (keep the receipt).

If payments are still due on an item, find out what they are and add them to the debts of the estate.

Finally, don't forget to add up any cash.

Salary

If the deceased was working at the time of death, there may be some unpaid salary or wages to come. Write and ask the employer for details of the amount, sending a death certificate. Other sums to enquire about include commission, profit shares and bonus.

Trade unions and professional associations often pay out death benefit to members who die in service (and occasionally in retirement). Write to the organisation's head office for details.

Pensions

If the deceased was a member of a pension scheme, or had a personal pension, there may be a lump sum on death. In most cases, any lump sum will be payable straight to the deceased's spouse or close family and will not become part of the estate. Write to the scheme administrator or pension provider for details.

If the deceased was already receiving a pension, there may be unpaid pension due. Ask the administrator or pension provider for details. With the state pension, there are details of how to claim unpaid pension in the pension book.

Note that many people are due pensions from more than one scheme, because of changing jobs during their career – make sure you chase them all up.

Income tax

If the deceased paid tax under PAYE (on wages, salary or pension), it's likely that there will be a tax rebate due to the estate. This is because the PAYE system spreads the tax-free allowances equally through the tax year, therefore anyone who dies before the end of the tax year will not have had the full allowances to which he/she is entitled.

And some people's estates will be entitled to reclaim tax paid on income from investments such as shares and unit trusts. If the deceased did not earn enough to pay income tax in the tax year of his/her death, any tax deducted from such investment income before it is paid out can be claimed back by the personal representatives.

Write to the Inspector in charge of the tax district which dealt with the deceased's affairs, with details of the death. As personal representative, you will receive a Tax Return for the deceased. Returning this will allow the taxman to work out how much tax rebate is due – this figure is needed for probate.

Note that in some cases, it may turn out that income tax is due on the deceased's estate. This is particularly likely if there was a lot of investment income not taxed at source, or the deceased was self-employed.

Debts

If anyone owed money to the deceased, these sums must be added to the value of the estate. This includes share dividends in the pipeline, loans to family or friends, pension due on the date of death and income tax repayments. It is a duty of the executors to collect these debts (unless the will includes provision for the debtor to be let off, or a bequest against which the debt can be set).

Money the deceased owed must be deducted from the estate, and repaid before the instructions of the will are carried out. Debts to watch out for include rates or poll tax, rent arrears or mortgage, gas or electricity bills, telephone or TV hire, hire purchase or credit payments, credit card debts or an overdraft. Many of these bills come in during the weeks after the death: you should let the organisations involved know of the death and tell them that they will be paid after probate is granted.

In some cases, there may be good reason to believe that there are people owed money who should be encouraged to put in a claim – where the deceased was in business, for example. Advertise for creditors if this is likely (see p24).

If debts owed are more than the estate is worth, then the estate is insolvent. Consult a solicitor immediately if this appears at all likely to be the case.

Savings accounts

Write to all banks, building societies, finance companies and any other institution the deceased saved with, asking for details of how much is in each account. Make sure the figure includes interest accrued to the account but not yet added: the sample letter opposite gives an example of how you might do this.

There are special procedures for some types of savings:

- National Savings (e.g. Income Bonds, Savings Certificates, Investment Account) – use form DNS904 to get details of all National Savings investments held by the deceased. Copies of the form are available from post offices

- Premium Bonds – these can remain in the draw for prizes while you seek probate, for up to a year after the death. Include them on form DNS904 when seeking details of other National Savings investments
- joint accounts – the deceased will be assumed to have owned half of joint accounts unless you can prove that he/she contributed more or less than half.

Life insurance policies

There are three important facts to establish about life insurance policies connected with the deceased:

- are they part of the estate?
- if they are, what are they worth?
- are they earmarked to repay a mortgage or other debt (i.e. legally charged to repay the loan)?

The first question isn't as straightforward as it may appear. For example, the deceased may have taken out a policy on his/her own life **written in trust** for someone else (children, for example). In this case, the insurance company can pay the proceeds direct to the beneficiaries without waiting for probate, and the money doesn't generally count as part of the deceased's estate. If a policy on the deceased's life isn't written in trust for someone else, the proceeds do count as part of the estate.

Dear Sir

Re: Alison Marilyn Brown deceased

I am executor of the will of the late Alison Marilyn Brown, who died on 7 April 1989. My co-executor is her daughter Beatrice Eleanor Cartwright of 17 Thresher Road, Slagthorpe, Borset. I enclose Mrs Brown's death certificate – please return this when you have noted it in your records.

The estate includes the asset described below. Please let me know the value of this asset at the date of death, including interest accrued but not yet added.

Particulars of asset
Name in which held: Mrs Alison Brown
Description of asset: Five Star Account
Reference number: 983270549
Estimated amount of value: £3,000

I should be grateful to know whether Mrs Brown had any other accounts with you and, if so, the balance at the date of death and the interest accrued to the date of death.

When the grant of probate has been obtained, I shall send an official copy of it to you for your inspection. Please let me know what formalities (if any) will be involved in obtaining payment of what is due to the estate.

Yours faithfully

A life insurance policy that the deceased had on the life of someone else (his/her spouse, say, or business partner) also counts as part of the estate. If the policy can be cashed in (often possible with whole life and endowment policies), the surrender value is added to the deceased's estate.

If there is a policy to be counted into the estate, the insurance company will tell you its value. In the case of a with-profits policy on the deceased's life, this may be much more than the basic sum insured, because bonuses have been added. But the surrender value of an endowment or whole life policy on someone else's life may be rather less, especially in the early years of a policy.

Where a policy is charged to an individual or organisation to pay off a loan, then the insurance company will pay it direct to the lender. If the amount paid out is more than the loan, the excess should be paid to the estate.

Stocks, shares and unit trusts

If there is any evidence that the deceased owned stocks, shares or unit trusts, you need to establish the amount of his/her holdings – there may be lost certificates, unclaimed rights issues or dividend or interest due. Write to the registrar of each company involved, using a letter similar to that below. You can find registrars' addresses in the *Register of Registrars* at a library, or by telephoning the companies.

There are special rules for valuing stocks and shares. If they are traded on the Stock Exchange, their value depends on the closing prices for the day of the death. These are recorded in the *Stock Exchange Daily Official List* for the day (see p32 for how to obtain a copy).

Two prices are quoted for each share: take the lower of the two prices and add a quarter of the difference between the higher price and the lower price. So if the

Dear Sir

The estate of Alison Marilyn Brown deceased – holding of 500 £1 ordinary shares in General Borset Traction PLC

I am executor of the will of the late Alison Marilyn Brown, who died on 7 April 1989. My co-executor is her daughter Beatrice Eleanor Cartwright of 17 Thresher Road, Slagthorpe, Borset.

I enclose Mrs Brown's death certificate – please return it when you have noted it in your records. I am in the course of preparing the papers for grant of probate and among the deceased's papers I have found the certificate for the above holding. I should be grateful if you would confirm to me the holding as above registered in the deceased's name, and also confirm that there are no unclaimed dividend, interest or other payments held at your offices.

I look forward to hearing from you as soon as possible, so that I can finalise the probate papers.

Yours faithfully

prices quoted are 100p and 104p, for example, the value is the lower price (100p), plus a quarter of the difference between the higher and lower price (104 – 100= 4p): that is, 100p + $^1/_4$ of 4p = 101p.

If the letter x is beside a share's price, this means that it has gone 'ex-dividend': the next dividend will be paid even though the shareholder has died. You will have to add the value of this dividend to the estate (the registrar of the company will tell you how much is due).

With unit trusts, their value is the lower of the two prices quoted for the day. Ask the unit trust management company for details of unit trust prices on the day of the death.

Valuing shares in private companies not traded on the Stock Exchange is a complicated matter (especially with family companies). If these are involved, you'll need expert help from an accountant or lawyer to agree their value with the Inland Revenue.

APPLYING FOR THE FORMS

Collecting together all the information can take some weeks. But you could go ahead and get the forms needed to seek probate or letters of administration before all the information is ready.

Write or telephone the personal application section of your nearest main Probate Registry, saying that you want to make a personal application. The addresses and telephone numbers are listed on sheet F in the back pocket of this Pack.

SECTION

3 INHERITANCE TAX

One of the objects of the probate process is to ensure that the right amount of inheritance tax is paid on the deceased's estate. Probate, or letters of administration, will not be granted until the inheritance tax bill is settled. This section outlines how inheritance tax works, how to work out the bill and how to raise the money to pay it. More detail is available in the Inland Revenue booklet IHT1: *Inheritance Tax*, available from the Capital Taxes Office (for addresses, see p32).

For most people, inheritance tax is not a problem – none is due on the majority of estates. For the rest, there will be inheritance tax to pay and dealing with it should not present a problem. But seek the advice of a solicitor or accountant if the deceased owned a farm, business or shares in a private company, or had dealings with private trusts. If the inheritance tax bill looks like being substantial, it might also be worth taking professional advice – it is often possible to rearrange estates to reduce tax.

HOW INHERITANCE TAX WORKS

Inheritance tax covers the estate of the person who has died. But it also covers gifts made in the seven years before death, so that people can't avoid the tax by giving things away shortly before they die. Certain other lifetime gifts also fall into the net (for example, gifts 'with reservation' – where the giver has retained the right to use what has been given away).

Many gifts and bequests are exempt from inheritance tax. For example, anything given to a husband or wife, or left to them on death, is free of inheritance tax. So are gifts and bequests to charity. And all sorts of smallish gifts made before death are exempt from inheritance tax, to avoid too much bureaucracy. There's a full list of all the exempt gifts and bequests opposite.

Once exempt gifts have been deducted, inheritance tax is due on the remaining total. The rate is nil% on the first slice of this total (£118,000 for the 1989–90 tax year). But the rate is 40% of every pound over the nil-rate slice.

For example, if the total is £150,000, the tax bill is worked out as follows:

The first £118,000 is taxed at nil%	£0
The next £32,000 is taxed at 40%	£12,800
Total inheritance tax	£12,800

The inheritance tax on gifts made before death has to be paid by the recipients. But if they received them more than three years before the death, their bill is scaled down on the following scale:

Years between gift and death	Percentage of full tax charge payable
Up to three	100%
More than three and up to four	80%
More than four and up to five	60%
More than five and up to six	40%
More than six and up to seven	20%

Gifts and bequests exempt from inheritance tax

The following gifts and bequests are exempt from inheritance tax whether made on death or in lifetime:

- between husband and wife (unless the recipient isn't domiciled in the UK)
- to UK registered charities
- to certain national institutions (e.g. the National Trust, British Museum)
- of certain types of *heritage property*
- of land in the UK to a registered housing association on or after 14 March 1989
- to political parties (within limits if made before 15 March 1988)
- shares in a company if given to a trust for the benefit of employees (provided certain conditions are met).

The following are exempt from inheritance tax only if made on death:

- lump-sum payments from pension schemes made at the discretion of the trustees (most are)
- refunds of personal pension contributions with interest paid directly to someone other than the personal representatives (e.g. a husband or wife)
- the estate of someone whose death was caused or hastened by active military service in war or of a warlike nature
- lump sums paid out by life insurance policies written in trust for someone else.

The following are exempt from inheritance tax only if made in lifetime:

- outright gifts to individuals made seven or more years before death
- small gifts of up to £250 to any number of different people in any one tax year
- gifts made as normal expenditure out of income (i.e. not from capital) – so long as the giver can keep up his/her normal standard of living after making the gifts
- gifts on marriage – each parent can give up to £5,000 tax-free in anticipation of the marriage, a grandparent or great-grandparent £2,500 and anyone else £1,000 (the gifts must be conditional on the marriage taking place)
- certain gifts for the maintenance of the giver's family (e.g. an ex-spouse, children under 18 or in full-time education, or infirm relatives)
- up to £3,000 a year of any other gifts (any unused part of this allowance can be carried over to the next tax year only).

Note that some lifetime gifts are liable to inheritance tax at the time the gift is made – mainly gifts to companies and certain types of trust. Gifts of this type can affect the inheritance tax payable on death up to 14 years later. This brief description of inheritance tax can't cover the complicated rules in theses cases – get professional advice if the deceased appears to have made such gifts.

Who pays the inheritance tax?

The inheritance tax on legacies made on death can be paid in one of two ways:

- the will can specify that the legacy is 'after tax'. In this case, the tax is paid by whoever gets the legacy – so if the legacy is £10,000, he or she would end

up with less than £10,000 if inheritance tax has to be paid
- alternatively, the will can make the legacy 'tax-free' (if nothing is said, it is assumed to be tax-free). In this case, the tax is paid by the estate, and if the legacy is £10,000, that is what the recipient gets.

Where a legacy is tax-free, the tax paid by the estate on the legacy forms part of the gift. If an estate is taxable and it includes a tax-free legacy of £10,000, this is in fact a legacy of £16,667: tax at 40% on £16,667 is £6,667 – leaving £10,000 to go tax-free to the legatee. Adding on the value of the tax is known as *grossing-up*: you simply multiply the value of the tax-free legacy by 100 and divide by 60.

Note that the calculation isn't quite so easy if part of the gift is taxable at the nil rate – this example assumes that the whole gift is taxable at 40%. If part of the estate is taxable at 40% and part at nil%, the average tax rate for the whole estate is used for grossing up.

WORKING OUT THE TAX BILL

In this section, we look at how the inheritance tax bill is normally worked out. You will need to estimate the bill: this will let you sort out the arrangements for paying the inheritance tax – essential before probate or letters of administration can be granted.

The first step is to add up any gifts made before death which are not exempt from inheritance tax (chargeable gifts). Most people won't have made any, since the sort of gifts they have made in lifetime are generally covered by the exemptions. Remember that outright gifts to individuals made seven or more years before death are exempt, as are gifts between husband and wife.

Next, add to the total of chargeable gifts, the chargeable value of the estate, i.e. the value excluding bequests which are exempt from inheritance tax. If the total is less than the maximum for the nil-rate band (£118,000 for 1989–90), there is no inheritance tax to pay.

If the total exceeds the nil-rate band, then inheritance tax is paid on the excess only – at a rate of 40%.

Example

Marilyn Brown, a widow, dies leaving an estate worth £140,000 (net of debts and expenses). She has made no taxable gifts in the previous seven years. She leaves £5,000 to charities and the residue of her estate to be divided between her three grown-up children.

The legacies to charity are free of inheritance tax. That leaves £140,000 – £5,000 = £135,000 of chargeable bequests for her three children. Inheritance tax on this £135,000 is worked out as follows:

£118,000 at nil%	£0
£17,000 at 40%	£6,800
Total inheritance tax	£6,800

That leaves £135,000 – £6,800 = £128,200 to be divided between the three children – ie £42,733 each.

PAYMENT OF INHERITANCE TAX

When you apply for probate or letters of administration, you will have to fill in various Inland Revenue forms to establish the inheritance tax liability of the estate (see p19). These will be used to draw up an Inland Revenue account, which you have to sign. A tax demand will be issued and must be paid before probate is granted.

In most cases, all the inheritance tax must be paid on demand. If it is paid more than six months after the death, interest is added from that date (at a rate linked to bank base rate).

But with some types of asset, the payment of inheritance tax can be spread over ten years. This applies to homes, buildings, land, a family business and certain unquoted shares. The concession applies only for as long as the assets are retained by the beneficiaries; if they are sold, all the tax is due right away.

On some assets such as farms and houses, the instalments are free of interest (unless they are paid late). With others such as a home, interest is charged on the unpaid tax. But it is likely to be cheaper to pay the interest on the instalments than to borrow the money to pay the tax in full. Even if you intend to pay off the inheritance tax once probate is granted, opting for instalments until probate could save a lot in interest.

FINANCE FOR INHERITANCE TAX

The inheritance tax bill must be sorted out *before* probate is granted. Yet the executors cannot get control of most of the money in the estate until *after* probate is granted. How can you pay the tax before getting your hands on the money in the estate?

Funds held in National Savings investments such as Savings Certificates, Premium Bonds, Investment Account and Income Bonds can be drawn upon to pay inheritance tax before probate. The Probate Registry can supply a note when you attend to swear the papers (see p21), which will allow the appropriate National Savings office to release the money needed to pay the tax. The money will be sent direct to the Probate Registry – and you can draw any balance when probate is granted.

Similar arrangements have been made by Girobank and many of the larger building societies. If such resources are not available – or are insufficient to cover the tax bill – you will need to approach a bank to lend the money.

The bank where the deceased had an account will normally agree to a loan, which can cover the inheritance tax and other expenses such as probate fees. An *executorship account* will be opened which can be used for any executor transactions (all executors will have to sign cheques).

A separate loan account will allow the executors to borrow the money for inheritance tax, to be paid out against cheques on the main account. There is tax relief on the interest on a loan for these purposes. Keeping a separate account makes the amount easy to identify.

Final adjustments

Payment of inheritance tax before grant of probate or letters of administration is not the last word of the Inland Revenue:

- home values are not agreed with the District Valuer until probate is granted
- valuation of unquoted shares similarly follows probate
- the executors may turn up a new asset (or find that an estimate was wrong), in which case the correction must be notified to the Inland Revenue.

And you may be able to reduce the inheritance tax bill if quoted stocks and shares are sold below their probate value within 12 months of the death. If the total proceeds before expenses of all stocks and shares sold in this period are less than their probate value, you can ask to have the inheritance tax based on the sale proceeds instead of the probate value.

After grant of probate or letters of administration, further adjustments may then be required before inheritance tax is finally settled (see p24).

SECTION

4 GETTING PROBATE

Once you have valued the estate and made the arrangements to pay inheritance tax, you can formally apply for grant of probate or letters of administration. Use the forms you should already have obtained from the Probate Registry (see p13).

In most cases, all that has to be done is to complete the forms and send them back to the main Probate Registry of your choice. Once they have been checked and passed, the personal representatives must swear a declaration in person at the Probate Registry. After probate fees and inheritance tax are paid, probate or letters of administration are granted.

The forms that you should have received are:

- PA1 – probate application form
- Cap 44 – return of assets and debts
- Cap 40 – schedule of stocks and shares
- Cap 37 – schedule of real, leasehold and immovable property
- PA5 – matrimonial home questionnaire.

In addition, you will get a guide to making a personal application for probate (PA2), a list of local probate offices (PA3), a table of the fees (PA4) and an envelope to return the forms in.

Form PA1

This form asks for details of:

- the local Probate Registry office you wish to use. Note when making your choice that some of the smaller offices are manned as little as once a month
- the deceased
- the will and any executors who cannot or will not act
- the surviving relatives
- the personal representatives making the application – the Registry will correspond with the top name.

Write your answers in the white sections only (the blue parts are for official use). You don't have to sign this form: it is used to prepare the oath you will later have to swear.

Form Cap 44

This is the main Inland Revenue form to list the contents of the estate (the other two 'Cap' forms ask for details of particular types of property). Your answers are used to prepare the Inland Revenue account for inheritance tax purposes (see p17). Use the answers on Checklists C, D and E to help you fill in Cap 44.

Cap 44 is fairly straightforward to complete, with useful instructions on what to enter (a new and more 'user-friendly' version is due to be introduced in 1990). You should have the answers gathered together from earlier work; if you are unsure what to enter, go back to the relevant pages in this Pack.

If there is insufficient space in any part of the form to enter all the details required, write them out on a separate sheet of paper, headed Schedule A (B, C etc). Then enter the grand total on Cap 44, with 'See Schedule A' (or whatever).

Section 1 of the current version of Cap 44 asks for details of assets and debts in the UK. Section 2 covers the same items outside the UK. Don't include in these first two Sections any jointly owned property (details of which must be entered later in the form).

If the deceased owned any stocks and shares, their total value is entered in Section 1. But don't give any details of the holdings (even if there is only one); these must be given on form Cap 40 (see below). Dividends in the pipeline (see p13) should be entered under Item 12 (*Other assets*).

The address and the value of freehold or leasehold property are entered under Item 15. Again, fuller details must be given on a separate form Cap 37 (see below).

After the listing of assets and liabilities, the remaining pages ask for other relevant information about the estate:

- details of jointly owned property
- property nominated to go direct to someone else (see p3)
- gifts made before death, which may fall into the inheritance tax net (see p14) You can leave out gifts within the limits set out on the form because these will be exempt from inheritance tax, but you must give details of any other 'transfer of value' (for example, something sold below its market value)
- details of any interests the deceased had in trusts
- payments made on the death from a pension scheme (these may not form part of the estate – see p9).

Form Cap 44 must be signed by all the personal representatives making the application for probate or letters of administration.

Form Cap 40

This form asks for a list of stocks, shares and unit trusts owned by the deceased. The information you have assembled on Checklist E will be all you need to fill this in, though you should put the holdings in the order they appear on the *Stock Exchange Official Daily List.*

The market value asked for on the form is worked out using the method described on page 12. Where a share was ex-dividend on the day of death, put 'xd' beside the market value.

Form Cap 37

Form Cap 37 is designed to cover many forms of real estate, including property let out, farmland and large estates. You will probably need to fill in only the details of the deceased's home, whether it was freehold or leasehold and its gross value (ignoring any mortgage which is entered as a debt on Cap 44). Enter the full value even if someone else is claiming a share of it.

You don't need to enter details of any property interest which has no capital value (a furnished tenancy, for example).

Form PA5

This form has to be filled in only if there is a widow or widower living in a home which was in the sole name of the deceased. It doesn't have to be filled in where the surviving spouse jointly owned the matrimonial home. Return it blank if it does not apply for the estate with which you are dealing.

If the form does apply, give details of whether the surviving spouse wishes to claim an interest in the property. You could do this if, for example, the survivor had provided some of the purchase price, contributed to the upkeep of the home or even put some work into it (renovating it, say).

You should also give an estimate of the percentage of the value of the home the survivor is claiming. The District Valuer may wish to negotiate on this figure (as may anyone else who is entitled to the rest of the value).

SENDING OFF THE FORMS

All the personal representatives making the application must sign form Cap 44, and should see the other forms before they are sent off. Also to be included are the original will (not a photocopy), the death certificate, schedules of assets summarised on the various forms and all the other forms even if blank.

Send your forms back to the main Probate Registry at which you wish to swear the forms. If you wish to use a local sub-office, send the papers back to the Probate Registry which controls it. Keep photocopies of all documents for your reference.

SWEARING THE FORMS

The Probate Registry will send you an appointment for swearing the papers, which involves all the personal representatives who have not withdrawn. Take along all papers connected with the probate application in case you need to prove a figure submitted.

The answers given on the various forms will have been converted into two legal documents:

- the executors' oath
- the Inland Revenue account.

You will all be asked to check every detail on both and sign them to signify that they are complete and accurate. You will all be asked to sign the original will as well.

You then swear on a copy of the New Testament that the oath is true, by repeating words spoken by the commissioner. You can opt for the Old Testament, or affirm if you have grounds for objecting to taking an oath. The ceremony is completed when the commissioner signs beneath each of the signatures on the oath and on the will.

After the oath has been sworn, the Probate Registry fee must be paid (see Box overleaf) – in cash, or by cheque, postal order or banker's draft. At the same time, you can order as many sealed copies of the grant of probate as you will need to wind up the estate (enough to send round the various bodies holding assets of the estate). Sealed copies cost 25p each and are embossed with the Court's seal to show that they are authoritative.

LETTERS OF ADMINISTRATION

The procedure for granting letters of administration is almost identical to that for probate. But occasionally, the administrators must provide a guarantee before letters are granted. This is usually needed only when the beneficiaries are under age or mentally disabled: the guarantee protects them from any harmful consequences of the administrators' failure. An insurance company should be able to provide a guarantee (for a fee). But if you can cover the full value of the estate yourself, no insurance guarantee is necessary.

Probate Registry fees

The fees depend on the net value of the estate (i.e. after paying off debts) for the purpose of inheritance tax, but excluding the value of any part of the estate which passes automatically to a surviving joint owner (e.g. a house owned under a joint tenancy).

Up to £10,000	maximum £10
£10,001–£25,000	a flat fee of £40 plus £1 for every £1,000 or part of £1,000
£25,001–£40,000	a flat fee of £80 plus £1 for every £1,000 or part of £1,000
£40,001–£70,000	a flat fee of £150 plus £1 for every £1,000 or part of £1,000
£70,001–£100,000	a flat fee of £215 plus £1 for every £1,000 or part of £1,000
£100,001 or more	a flat fee of £300 for the first £200,000 plus £50 for each additional £100,000 or part of £100,000 plus £1 for every £1,000 of the estate (or part of £1,000)

Example

Estate of £264,432:

Flat rate fee for the first £200,000	£300
The next £100,000 (or part)	£50
For the 265 x £1,000 (or part)	£265
TOTAL	£615

THE GRANT

If inheritance tax is due on the estate, a tax demand will be sent about two to three weeks after the oath is sworn. Grant of probate or letters of administration will follow payment of inheritance tax a week or two later (and if there is no tax to pay, will be made a week or two after the oath is sworn). In some cases, there may be a delay over valuation or some other technicality with probate, in which case a further visit to the Registry may be called for.

The grant comes with the sealed copies you ordered and a copy of the will (the original is lodged at Somerset House in London).

SECTION

ADMINISTERING THE ESTATE

Once probate or letters of administration are granted, the personal representatives can get on with administering the estate. You can now collect in all the assets of the estate, pay its debts and begin to distribute the bequests.

It could make sense to wait six months after the grant before distributing any major assets. This is the deadline for anyone who wishes to claim a share of the estate under the Inheritance (Provision for Family and Dependants) Act 1975 – on the grounds that he/she was partly or wholly maintained by the deceased (see p3). If you are certain that no such claims will arise, you can go ahead.

COLLECTING IN CASH

Send sealed copies of the grant to everyone who holds an asset belonging to the estate, asking for it be sent to you as personal representatives. The letter illustrated below should be adapted as appropriate for:

- bank, building society and other savings accounts (including National Savings)
- life insurance companies
- the deceased's former employer or pension fund administrator
- the Inspector of Taxes, where a refund of income tax is due or tax is owed by the estate
- the Department of Social Security for state pension arrears
- dividends due on shares.

Each organisation which owes money to the estate will need to see a sealed copy of the grant to register it before paying out. It may also stamp the copy on the back.

Dear Sir

Re: Alison Marilyn Brown deceased

I now enclose a sealed copy of the probate of the will. I should be glad if you could return it to me when you have recorded details.

Please now close the deceased's Five Star Account at your branch and transfer the money in it to the executorship account in my name and that of my co-executor Beatrice Cartwright, at the National Barminster Bank, 43 High Street, Slagthorpe, Borset (account number: 10966543).

Yours faithfully

PAYING THE DEBTS

Calling in all the cash may provide enough to settle the deceased's debts (if not, see below for selling assets to raise more money). These debts can now be settled – ask for receipts for your records.

If you need to advertise for unknown creditors, now is the time to do so. In many cases you will not need to, because you know that there are no debts owed by the deceased of which you are not aware. But if someone turns up later with a justifiable claim, the personal representatives would have to pay the debt out of their own pockets.

You can cover yourself against this by advertising for creditors, setting a two-month deadline for applications, in the *London Gazette* and a newspaper in the area where the dead person held property. There is a standard format, including the name and address of the person creditors should apply to and the closing date – you can use Oyez forms to place the advertisements (see p32). The *London Gazette* won't accept a notice before probate is granted except from a solicitor, but you can go ahead earlier with a local paper.

Form Cap 30

At this stage, some final adjustments in the inheritance tax bill may be needed (see p17). A further return may have to be signed and additional tax paid as a result of these items.

When you feel certain that everything has been settled for inheritance tax, ask the Capital Taxes Office for two copies of Form Cap 30. Complete and return them – all the executors must sign. One copy will be stamped and returned to you if all is in order.

No further inheritance tax can then be demanded except in cases of fraud, or where you have failed to disclose an important fact, or the will's provisions are varied in a way that increases the tax liability. Until Cap 30 is returned, it would be unwise to wind up the estate completely – the personal representatives would have to find any more inheritance tax from their own pockets. Cap 30 won't be issued until every penny of tax is paid – though if you are paying by instalments, a certificate will be issued 'save and except the property on which tax is being paid by instalments' which allows you to go ahead.

SELLING OFF ASSETS

At this stage, there will be assets such as shares, unit trusts and the deceased's home which have to be dealt with. Some of these may be specifically bequeathed to particular people, and so long as this leaves enough to cover debts and cash legacies, you can arrange the transfers.

If assets aren't specifically bequeathed – or there isn't enough money to pay the debts and cash legacies – you will have to consider selling some or all of them. Discuss this with the residuary legatees, the people who will get whatever's left at the end of the process. For example, they might prefer to keep one lot of investments themselves, or to retain the deceased's home for holiday use.

Stocks, shares and unit trusts

You can sell stocks and shares through a bank or stockbroker who will supply the necessary forms. You hand over the share certificates plus a sealed copy of the grant for each company registrar to show that you are entitled to sell them. All the personal representatives have to sign the sale forms.

If the shares are to be transferred to beneficiaries of the will (instead of sold), you can do this yourself, using stock transfer form Con 40 from Oyez Stationery (see p32). A form is needed for each stock or share, and each company registrar will need to see a sealed copy of the grant of probate. There will be a fee to pay for registering the change of ownership (but stamp duty is no longer payable on such a transfer – choose the appropriate reason on the back of Con 40 to claim exemption).

If you are dividing stocks and shares between the residuary legatees, the simplest way is to divide each shareholding equally between them. If you allocate the shares in one company to one legatee and those of another company to the second, then you will have to value the shares again to make sure that the legatees have received the proportion of the estate they are entitled to. If the shares have to be valued for this reason, take the mid-price between the higher and lower prices on the day of distribution (if a share is ex-dividend, the dividend goes to the estate).

Note that where shares are bequeathed to you and you are sole personal representative, no formal transfer of shares is needed. You can register your name as shareholder simply by completing a letter of request (form Con 41A from Oyez Stationery – see p32).

Unit trust sales or transfers have to be organised through the management company. Again, they will need a sealed copy of the grant.

There may be an adjustment to the inheritance tax bill if shares and unit trusts are sold within a year of the death for less than their value at death (see p18).

The home

The deceased's home cannot be sold until the grant of probate or letters of administration. But it may be possible to put it on the market before, so long as any interested buyers are told that the sale cannot proceed until the grant. The solicitor or whoever handles the legal side of the sale will have to take extra steps after the grant to establish that you have the authority to sell the home.

If the home is to be transferred to a beneficiary, this too must await the grant. The exact procedure for carrying out the transfer depends on whether the home is registered or unregistered property (i.e. whether it has been registered with the Land Registry) – the details are below.

This procedure must be followed even with joint ownership as tenants in common. With joint ownership as joint tenants, there are no transfer papers to complete. The death certificate is enough to establish the survivor's title and should be placed with the deeds (unregistered property) or sent to the Land Registry (registered property).

Registered property

Where there was no mortgage on the dead person's home, you will need to find the *land certificate*, which is formal proof of ownership. If this cannot be found, you will have to apply to the Land Registry for another.

Where a mortgage is still outstanding, the loan will first have to be repaid. The letter at the top of the next page indicates how you might do this.

The lender will give you the charge certificate, together with an official acknowledgement that the loan is repaid (often on Land Registry form 53). Send

Dear Sir

Re: Alison Marilyn Brown deceased, 33 Acacia Avenue, Slagthorpe, Borset - Mortgage No. 77/192837465

I now enclose a sealed copy of the probate of the will. I should be glad if you could return it to me when you have recorded details.

Further to your letter, I enclose £7,434.33 and should be grateful if you will arrange for the mortgage to be discharged. Please send all the deeds and documents to me, together with the official certificate of discharge.

Until the house is sold, we wish to maintain the existing insurance policy for the building. Please arrange this and let me know if any formalities are required (or further premium).

Yours faithfully

these to the Land Registry which will cross out the details of the mortgage and issue the land certificate.

There are two other steps to be achieved:

- registering the grant with the Land Registry by sending a sealed copy – the personal representatives become the registered owners
- transferring the home into the name of the beneficiary – use Land Registry form 56 from HMSO or Oyez (see p32), sending the appropriate fee.

If you've already got the land certificate, you can send it off with the grant and form 56 to achieve these two steps together. If you haven't yet had the mortgage crossed off, you can do this at the same time as the two steps above – the letter below indicates how you might do this. After some weeks, the Land Registry will send back the grant and the new land certificate in the name of the beneficiary.

With leasehold property, the landlord must be informed of the changes. The

Dear Sir

The Larches, Ivy Lane, Borminster Newton, Borset - BO2121212

I enclose a sealed copy of the probate of Harold David Bean's will, the charge certificate for The Larches, Ivy Lane, forms 53 and 56 and a cheque payable to HM Land Registry for £60.

Please cancel the mortgage and register Mary Diana Peggotty as the new owner.

Please then return the copy of the probate and the land certificate to Ms Peggotty.

Yours faithfully

lease may require the landlord to be sent a copy of form 56 and even paid a fee.

Details of the transfer should be written or typed on the back of the original grant of probate – see the example memo, below. This gives the beneficiary the right to produce the grant at some date in the future as evidence that the home is his or hers.

Memo: An assent dated 30 January 1990 vested the freehold house The Larches, Ivy Lane, Borminster Newton, Borset in Mary Diana Peggotty, and her right to the production of this grant of probate was acknowledged.

Note that if the will leaves the home to an executor, it still has to be re-registered following both the above steps: first registering the executor, then transferring it to the same person as an individual.

Unregistered property

Ownership of a home which is not registered at the Land Registry is established from its deeds (if there is a mortgage, the lender will have these). It is not quite as easy for a lay person to handle the transfer of unregistered property with confidence partly because there is no form back from the Land Registry to confirm that the transfer has been accomplished. But unless there are complications or the mortgage is not paid off, you can carry out the transfer by drawing up an *assent*, like the one overleaf, on a sheet of paper.

The assent should be signed in the presence of a witness, who must also sign it, adding his/her address and occupation. No stamp duty is needed. The assent must be stored with the deeds.

With a leasehold home, details of the lease should appear in the assent. The landlord should be notified, and may be entitled to a copy of the assent and a fee.

Again, write or type a note about the transfer on the back of the original grant of probate – see the example memo, on this page. This gives the beneficiary the right to produce the grant at some date in the future as evidence that the home is his/hers.

Capital gains tax

Shares or unit trusts sold by the personal representatives may produce a capital gains tax bill for the estate. So, too, may a home or any other asset if not exempt from capital gains tax.

If the assets are worth more on disposal than when the owner died, the difference, after allowing for inflation, is the capital gain (if they are worth less, then a loss is incurred). If net taxable gains (i.e. less taxable losses) exceed a certain level in a tax year (£5,000 for the 1989–90 tax year), there is capital gains tax to pay on the excess. But note that if the administration continues after the end of the second full tax year after the death, capital gains tax is payable on the whole of the chargeable gain – there is no exemption.

INCOME TAX

The estate must pay tax on its income like any other taxpayer, at the basic rate of 25%. There are no tax-free allowances for the income of the estate (though there is also no higher rate tax at 40%). Interest the estate pays on loans to pay inheritance tax qualifies for tax relief (see p17).

The personal representatives will be sent a special Tax Return R59, normally when they apply to the Inland Revenue for the dead person's tax rebates. This has to be completed for each tax year or part tax year that the administration continues (tax years run from 6 April in one year to 5 April in the following year).

You don't need to enter income on the Tax Return if it is paid after tax (for example, share dividends with tax credits, bank and building society interest). But if you have taken out a loan to pay inheritance tax, you may need to claim back some of the tax paid on share dividends and unit trust distributions as your tax relief. To reclaim this tax, you will need the tax credits on the counterfoils attached to the dividend or distribution payments. (Note that you can't claim back the 'composite rate tax' deducted from bank and building society interest.)

You will also have to give details on the Tax Return of capital gains made – for example, on shares and unit trusts (see above). Attach a schedule of all the individual holdings, when they were sold, their value on form Cap 44 and the proceeds of the sales (after fees etc), summarising the total gain on the Return.

The administration ends when all the assets and debts have been found out and paid over. You don't have to wait until the assets have been distributed before dealing with income tax.

ASSENT

We hereby assent to the freehold property The Larches, Ivy Lane, Borminster Newton, Borset vesting in Mary Diana Peggotty of The Larches, Ivy Lane, Borminster Newton, Borset.

We make this assent as executors of the will of Mr Harold David Bean, who died on 12 June 1989.

Probate of his will was granted to us by the Principal Probate Registry on 1 October 1989.

We hereby acknowledge Mary Diana Peggotty's right to the production of probate.

Dated 30 January 1990

Signed by the executors of the will of Harold David Bean deceased:

William McGregor of 47 High Street, Slagthorpe, Borset, teacher, and Melanie Templeman of The Old Farm, Mill Lane, Borminster Newton, Borset, journalist.

Signatures:

Witness:

SECTION

WINDING UP THE ESTATE

When you are certain that there are no further claimants or debtors to be dealt with, you can make the final distribution of assets. Once this is done, there are a few simple steps to follow before the business is concluded.

DISTRIBUTION OF ASSETS

Any bequests and legacies in the will should now be carried out:

- ask all beneficiaries for a simple receipt when handing over cash (see below for example)

> **Alison Marilyn Brown deceased**
>
> **I acknowledge that I have received the sum of one thousand pounds (£1,000) from Henry A. Brown and Beatrice E. Cartwright in settlement of the legacy due to me under the will of the late Alison Marilyn Brown.**
>
> **Dated 6 December 1989**
>
> **Signed:**

- where an object (such as an heirloom or antique) is left to someone, ask him/her to sign an acknowledgement that he/she has received it (see example, right).

Beneficiaries under 18 cannot legally give a receipt, and could (in theory) come and demand a bequest again when reaching 18. Many wills leaving bequests to under-18s now include words to the effect that 'the receipt of the parent shall be sufficient discharge'. In this case, you can hand over the bequest in return for an appropriate receipt signed by the parent on behalf of the child.

Where there is no provision for the parent to acknowledge receipt, the executors should hold on to the bequest until the child reaches 18. Money should be invested in a trustee account on behalf of the child, to earn interest. A National Savings Investment Account is often used for this as it pays interest without deduction of tax: the child would have to pay tax only if his/her income was more than the personal allowance (£2,785 for the 1989–90 tax year).

If the administration of an estate continues for more than a year after the

> **Alison Marilyn Brown deceased**
>
> **I acknowledge that I have received the water colour portrait of Sir Stamford Raffles by Valentine Thursby left to me under the will of the late Alison Marilyn Brown.**
>
> **Dated 7 December 1989**
>
> **Signed:**

death, beneficiaries who get cash legacies are entitled to interest. The rate is six % a year, and it runs from the one year anniversary; the money comes from the estate (which should be earning interest on it anyway).

THE ACCOUNTS OF THE ESTATE

After all the specific bequests and legacies have been paid out, what's left is the residue. Before this is distributed, one last and very thorough check is necessary to make sure that every debt has been paid and every request in the will carried out.

Then you should draw up accounts to present to the person or people who get the residue – *the residuary legatee(s)*. The latter can check that they have received their dues and, by signing the accounts, give the personal representatives approval for winding up the estate.

Opposite is an example set of accounts for a fictitious estate:

- the **capital account** lists the value of the estate on death, plus any gains made on assets in the estate (on stocks and shares). The total is the amount available to cover debts, expenses and legacies – anything left over is available for distribution to the residuary legatees
- the **income account** lists the income of the estate (interest on deposits, say), with expenses paid by the estate (on the executors' loan, say), with any refundable tax paid itemised separately
- the **distribution account** sets out how the total available for distribution (from the capital account and income account) is actually divided up.

The amount of money left to be distributed to the residuary legatees should match what you now have left – if not, check the figures.

The accounts must be signed by the personal representatives and the residuary legatees, and kept with all the other administration papers for 12 years. If life interests in trusts are created by the will, the papers should be kept for 12 years after the death of anyone with a life interest.

THE RESIDUARY LEGATEE(S) AND TAX

Some of the residue may be income earned by the estate, on which income tax has been paid. That income becomes part of the income of the beneficiary for the tax year in which it is paid to him/her.

He/she will not have to pay basic rate tax on this income, since it has already been paid by the estate. If the residuary legatee's income is too low to pay tax, he/she will be able to claim back the income tax deducted. If he/she pays tax at the higher rate of 40%, extra tax will be due on it.

The personal representatives should hand over income tax deduction certificates to the residuary legatees with details of the tax paid. Inland Revenue form R185E should be used.

To work out the tax deducted, the net (after-tax) income must be grossed-up to find the gross (before-tax) income – the difference is the tax deducted. If the basic rate of tax is 25%, income is grossed up by multiplying it by

$$\frac{100}{100-25} = \frac{100}{75} = 1.33$$

So if the net income is £100, the gross income is 1.33 x £100 = £133.33 – and the tax paid is £33.33.

The estate of Alison Marilyn Brown deceased

Estate accounts for the period of administration
Date of death: 7 April 1989
Date administration completed: 19 December 1989

CAPITAL ACCOUNT		
receipts	£	£
Assets at date of death		
Property – 33 Acacia Avenue	118,500.00	
less mortgage	6,968.44	111,531.56
Contents of home		5,835.00
Life insurance policy, Slagthorpe Equitable		9,564.00
Premium bonds		220.00
Building society		3,264.76
Current account National Borminster Bank		674.89
Cash		34.12
Deposit account		5,147.32
National Savings Investment Account		452.68
Stocks and shares (as on Cap 44)		3,467.56
Pension from Slagthorpe Borough Council	42.57	
State retirement pension	35.98	78.55
Income tax repayment		65.44
Gain on stocks and shares sold since death		5.73
Total receipts		140,341.61
payments		
Debts at date of death		227.06
Funeral account paid		754.75
Probate fees		445.00
Inheritance tax paid		7,964.78
House sale expenses		2,350.00
Bank charges for selling shares		20.00
Legacies paid		5,000.00
Balance to distribution account		123,580.02
Total payments		140,341.61

INCOME ACCOUNT	gross	tax credit	net
receipts	£	£	£
National Savings Investment Account	21.94		21.94
Share dividend	205.64	51.41	154.23
Building society interest			86.75
Tax repayment on executors' loan		33.11	33.11
Total tax credit in estate		18.30	
Balance from distribution account			391.63
Total receipts			687.66
payments			
Interest on executors' loan acount			132.43
Interest on mortgage			465.89
Executors' expenses			89.34
Total payments			687.66

DISTRIBUTION ACCOUNT	
receipts	
From capital account, balance for distribution	123,580.02
less deficit from income account	391.63
Total receipts	123,188.39
payments	
To Alexandra Caroline Jones	41,062.80
To Beatrice Eleanor Cartwright	41,062.80
To Phillip Anthony Brown	41,062.79
Total payments	123,188.39

Approved (signatures of residuary legatees plus executors)

USEFUL ADDRESSES

For a list of main Probate Registries and local probate offices, see insert F in the back pocket of this Pack.

Inland Revenue Capital Taxes Offices

England and Wales:
Minford House
Rockley Road
London W14 0DF
Tel 01-603 4622

Scotland:
16 Picardy Place
Edinburgh EH1 3NB
Tel 031-556 8511

N. Ireland:
Law Courts Building
Chichester Street
Belfast BT1 3NU
Tel 0232-235111

The London Gazette

51 Nine Elms Lane
London SW8 5DR
Tel 01-873 8359

The Stock Exchange Daily Official List

Back editions are available, price £9.25 (including postage), from:

Publications Department
The International Stock Exchange
London EC2N 1HP
Tel 01-588 2355

Oyez shops

Many useful law forms for probate can be bought from Oyez Stationery shops, with branches in Birmingham, Bradford, Cardiff, Exeter, Leeds, Liverpool, Manchester and Sheffield in addition to three in London. There are also seven tele-sales offices; the London sales office telephone number is 01-407 1982.

The most useful forms are:

Powers of attorney (p7)
Pro 6 – For an executor to give power of attorney
Pro 10 – For an administrator to give power of attorney

Renunciation of administration/ executorship (p7)
Pro 30 – For an administrator to renounce, where there is a will
Pro 3 – For an administrator to renounce, where there is no will
Pro 31A – For an executor to renounce

Advertising for claimants (p24)
Pro 36A – For advertising in the *London Gazette*
Pro 36C – For advertising in *The Times, Daily Telegraph, The Guardian, Yorkshire Post* or *Birmingham Post*
Pro 36B – For advertising in other newspapers

Transfer of stocks and shares (p25)
Con 40 – Stock transfer form
Con 41A – Stock transfer to a personal representative

Land Registry (p26)
LR 56 – For transferring a home to a beneficiary of a will

MAIN PROBATE REGISTRIES AND LOCAL OFFICES –ADDRESSES

MAIN PROBATE REGISTRY	LOCAL OFFICES
BANGOR 1st Floor, Bron Castell, High Street, Gwynedd LL57 1YS Tel: (0248) 362410	
BIRMINGHAM 3rd Floor, Cavendish House, Waterloo Street B2 5PS Tel: 021-236 4560/6263	**Coventry:** Ground Floor, Combined Court Centre, 140 Much Park Street **Kidderminster:** Crown House (Entrance D) **Lichfield:** Beaconsfield House, Sandford Street **Northampton**: St. Katherine's House, 21-27 St. Katherine's Street **Wolverhampton**: Bond House, St Johns Square
BODMIN Market Street PL31 2JW Tel: (0208) 72279	**Penzance**: County Court Building, Trevear, Alverton **Plymouth**: 5th Floor, Pearl Assurance Building, Royal Parade **Truro**: 1st Floor, Eagle Star House, 74-75 Lemon Street
BRIGHTON William Street BN2 2LG Tel: (0273) 684071	**Crawley**: 6thFloor, Sussex House, High Street

MAIN PROBATE REGISTRY	LOCAL OFFICES
	Hastings: Law Courts, Bohemia Road **Tunbridge Wells**: Merevale House, 42-46 London Road **Worthing**: Teville Gate House, Railway Approach
BRISTOL: The Crescent Centre, Temple Back BS1 6EP Tel: (0272) 273915/24619	**Bath**: Ham Gardens House, Ham Gardens **Taunton**: Room 330, Entrance C, Brendon House, Upper High Street **Weston-Super-Mare**: Lloyds Bank Chambers, High Street
CARLISLE 2 Victoria Place CA1 1ER Tel: (0228) 21751	**Workington**: Langdale House, Gray Street
CARMARTHEN 14 King Street, Dyfed SA31 1BL Tel: (0267) 236238	**Aberystwyth**: 30 Pier Street **Haverfordwest**: c/o P.S.A. Area Office, Winch Lane **Swansea**: 5th Floor, Ty Nant, High Street
CHESTER 5th Floor, Hamilton House, Hamilton Place, CH1 2DA Tel:(0224) 45082	**Rhyl**: The New Lessor Building, 64 Brighton Road Wrexham: 2nd Floor, 31 Chester Street

MAIN PROBATE REGISTRY	LOCAL OFFICES
EXETER Eastgate House, High Street EX4 3JZ Tel: (0392) 74515	**Barnstaple**: 7th Floor, Civic Centre, North Walk **Newton Abbot**: Bridge House, Courtenay Street **Yeovil**: 20 Kingston
GLOUCESTER 3 Pitt Street GL1 2BJ Tel: (0452) 22585	**Cheltenham**: The Court House, County Court Road, (Off Regent Street) **Hereford**: 1A St Johns Street **Worcester**: Shire Hall, Foregate Street
IPSWICH Level 3 Haven House, 17 Lower Brook Street IP4 1DN Tel: (0473) 253724	**Chelmsford**: London House, New London Road **Colchester**: Falklands House, 25 South Way
LANCASTER Mitre House, Church Street LA1 1HE Tel: (0524) 36625	**Barrow-in-Furness**: Rooms 205/206, 2nd Floor, Furness House, Schneider Square **Blackpool**: Room 118, 22 Plymouth Road **Preston**: 4th Floor, Red Rose House, 104 Lancaster Road
LEEDS 3rd Floor, Coronet House, Queen Street LS1 2BK Tel: (0532) 431505	**Bradford**: 3rd Floor, Forster House, Forster Square **Harrogate**: Berkeley House, 35 Victoria Avenue

MAIN PROBATE REGISTRY	LOCAL OFFICES
	Huddersfield: Crown Court Building, Princess Street **Wakefield**: Entrance B, Crown House, Kirkgate
LEICESTER Government Buildings, Newarke Street LE1 5SE Tel: (0533) 546117	**Bedford**: 29 Goldington Road **Kettering**: Northampton House, Station Road
LINCOLN Mill House, Brayford Side North LN1 1YW Tel: (0522) 23648	**Grimsby**: Grimsby Combined Court Centre, Town Hall Square
LIVERPOOL 3rd Floor, India Buildings, Water Street L2 OQR Tel: (051) 236 8264	**Southport**: Room 019, 1st Floor, Dukes House, Hogton Street **St Helens**: Crown Buildings, College Street **Wallasey**: Ground Floor, Dominick House, St Albans Road
LLANDAFF Probate Registry of Wales, 49 Cardiff Road, Llandaff, Cardiff CF5 2YW Tel: (0222) 562422	**Bridgend**: Crown Buildings, (Ground Floor, County Court), Angel Street **Newport (Gwent)**: 8th Floor, Olympia House, Dock Street **Pontypridd**: 2nd Floor, A.E.U. House, Sardis Road

MAIN PROBATE REGISTRY	LOCAL OFFICES
LONDON Principal Registry of the Family Division 2nd Floor, Somerset House, Strand, London WC2R 1LP Tel: 01-936 6983	**Croydon:** 5th Floor, Concord House, 454 London Road (near Mayday Road), West Croydon **Edmonton**: The Court House, 2nd Floor, 59 Fore Street, Upper Edmonton **Harlow**: 1st Floor, Gate House, The High **Kingston-Upon-Thames**: 1st Floor, Drapers Court, Kingston Hall Road **Luton**: Room 4, 2nd Floor, Cresta House, Alma Street **Romford**: 1st Floor, Lloyds Bank Chambers, 185a South Street **Southend-on-Sea**: 3rd Floor, (County Court Office), South Wing, Metropolitan House, 33 Victoria Avenue **Watford**: Room 301, 3rd Floor, Oxford House, 40 Clarendon Road **Woolwich**: 2nd Floor, Crown Building, Woolwich New Road
MAIDSTONE The Law Courts Barker Road ME18 8EW Tel: (0622) 54966	**Canterbury**: 22/23 St Margaret's Street **Chatham**: Anchorage House, High Street **Folkestone**: Palting House, Trinity Road

MAIN PROBATE REGISTRY	*LOCAL OFFICES*
MANCHESTER 9th Floor, Astley House, 23 Quay Street M3 4AT Tel: (061) 834 4319	**Bolton**: Room 010, 56-61 Bradshawgate **Burnley**: Room 409, 4th Floor, Brun House, Kingsway **Oldham**: Prudential Buildings, 79 Union Street **Stockport**: 4th Floor, Heron House, Wellington Street **Warrington**: Room 330, Hilden House, 103 Sankey Street **Wigan**: Wigan County Court, Crawford Street
MIDDLESBROUGH 12/16 Woodlands Road TS1 3BE Tel: (0642) 244770	**Darlington**: Bondgate House, 90 Bondgate **Durham**: Elvet House, Hallgarth Street
NEWCASTLE-UPON-TYNE 2nd Floor, Plummer House, Croft Street NE1 6NP Tel: 091-2618383	**Morpeth**: 17 Market Place **Sunderland**: Dunn House, North Bridge Street
NORWICH Combined Court Building The Law Courts, Bishopsgate, NR3 1UR Tel: (0603) 761776	**Lowestoft**: Lyndhurst, 28 Gordon Road

MAIN PROBATE REGISTRY	LOCAL OFFICES
NOTTINGHAM Upper Ground Floor, Lambert House, Talbot Street, NG1 5NR Tel: (0602) 414288	**Derby**: Combined Court Centre, Morledge **Mansfield**: 1st Floor, 39 Stockwell Gate
OXFORD 10A New Road OX1 1LY Tel: (0865) 241163	**Aylesbury**: Heron House, 49 Buckingham Street **Banbury**: 1st Floor, County Court, 35 Parson's Street **High Wycombe**: County court, Law Courts, Easton Street **Reading**: 1st Floor, County Court, 10 Friars Walk, Friar Street **Slough**: 1st Floor, Prudential Buildings, High Street **Swindon**: 1st Floor, The Law Courts, Islington Street
PETERBOROUGH Clifton House, Broadway PE1 1SL Tel: (0733) 62802	**Cambridge**: County Court Offices, 72/80 Hills Road **Kings Lynn**: Crown Court Buildings, College Lane
SHEFFIELD The Court House, Castle Street S3 8LW Tel: (0742) 729920	**Chesterfield**: 49 Church Way **Doncaster**: 1st Floor, Kingsway House, Hallgate

MAIN PROBATE REGISTRY	*LOCAL OFFICES*
STOKE-ON-TRENT 2nd Floor, Town Hall, Albion Street, Hanley ST1 1QL Tel: (0782) 213736	**Crewe**: 6 Nile Street **Shrewsbury**: Mardol House, Claremont Street **Stafford**: 2nd Floor, New Oxford House, 25 Greengate Street
WINCHESTER 4th Floor, Cromwell House, Andover Road SO23 7EW Tel: (0962) 53046/63771	**Basingstoke**: 3rd Floor, Brook House, Alencon Link **Bournemouth**: Crown Chambers, Richmond Hill **Dorchester**: Crown Building, (Room 25) Bridport Road **Guildford**: Law Courts (2nd Floor), Mary Road **Newport (Isle of Wight)**: Broadlands House **Portsmouth**: Combined Court Centre, Courts of Justice,Winston Churchill Avenue **Salisbury**: Alexandra House, New Street **Southampton**: Combined Court Centre, Courts of Justice, London Road
YORK Duncombe Place YO1 2EA Tel: (0904) 24210	**Hull**: 4th Floor, Commerce House, Paragon Street **Scarborough**: 9 Northway

FREEPOST

DEPARTMENT SORT OUT WILL

CONSUMERS' ASSOCIATION

P.O. BOX 44

HERTFORD SG14 1YB

Thank you for buying this Pack. We hope you find it useful. Below is a list of loose elements it should contain. Please check your copy now. If you find anything missing please tick the relevant box and we will send you a replacement.

- A ☐ *Sorting Out Someone's Will The Essential Steps*
- B ☐ *Sorting Out a Will Progress Checklist*
- C ☐ *Possessions Checklist*
- D ☐ *Savings and Investments Checklist*
- E ☐ *Stocks, Shares and Unit Trust Checklist*
- F ☐ *Main Probate Registries and Local Offices*

PLEASE USE BLOCK CAPITALS

Name ____________

Address ____________

____

____________ **Postcode** ____________

Date purchased ____________ **from**

Consumers' Association ☐ **Store** ☐

Store name ____________

Town ____________

Income Tax (page 29)

The Chancellor proposed to raise the personal allowance for income tax from £3,005 for the 1990-91 tax year to £3,295 for the 1991-92 tax year.

September 1991 a/s 207

HOW TO SORT OUT SOMEONE'S WILL

Inheritance Tax
In his Budget speech, the Chancellor proposed to raise the threshold for Inheritance Tax from £128,000 to £140,000. The rate of tax remains at 40 per cent.

Capital Gains Tax (page 27)
The annual exemption from capital gains tax has been increased from £5,000 to £5,500.

Income Tax (page 29)
The Chancellor proposed to raise the personal allowance for income tax from £3,305 for the 1990-91 tax year to £3,295 for the 1991-92 tax year.

SORTING OUT A WILL – PROGRESS CHECKLIST

Tick each box as step is completed.

Even if you decide to seek professional advice, use this Checklist to monitor progress.

- Register the death (p6) ☐
- Find the will (p6) ☐
- Sort out who will act as executor(s), or administrators if no executors are appointed by the will (p7) ☐
- Collect details of the assets and liabilities of the estate (p7) ☐
- Arrange insurance for any valuable assets if necessary (p8) ☐
- Send off for the probate forms from the Probate Registry (p13) ☐
- When all details of the estate are collected, check that there is enough to pay debts and legacies (P10) ☐
- Arrange funds to pay the inheritance tax (p17) ☐
- Complete and return the Probate Registry forms (p19) ☐
- Swear the oath at the Probate Registry and pay probate fees (p21) ☐
- Pay the inheritance tax (p22) ☐
- Receive grant of probate or letters of administration (p22) ☐
- Advertise for creditors if necessary (p24) ☐
- Use the grant to collect in assets (p23) ☐
- Agree value of home with the District Valuer (p17) ☐
- Sort out income tax and capital gains tax for the estate (p28) ☐
- Pay any outstanding inheritance tax and get Form 30 (p24) ☐
- Pay debts (p24) ☐
- Carry out bequests and legacies (p29) ☐
- Check that no claims exist on the estate (p31) ☐
- Prepare the estate accounts and agree them with the residuary legatees (p31) ☐
- Distribute the residue (p31) ☐

UNQUOTED SHARES

Type	Unit	Number held	Value (take professional advice)

VALUE OF UNPAID DIVIDENDS

Stock or share	Number held	Dividend per share	Amount owed

STOCKS, SHARES AND UNIT TRUSTS CHECKLIST

Enter details overleaf, filling in valuations as you complete them.

Enter details of possessions on Checklist C.
For other investments, see Checklist D.

BRITISH GOVERNMENT STOCK

Type	Unit	A Number held	B Lower selling price	C Higher buying price	D Difference between buying price C and selling price B	E Probate value = selling price B + $\frac{1}{4}$ difference D	Total value of holding (A x E)

OTHER FIXED INTEREST STOCK (EG LOCAL AUTHORITY, FOREIGN GOVERNMENT)

Type	Unit	A Number held	B Lower selling price	C Higher buying price	D Difference between buying price C and selling price B	E Value = lower selling price B + $\frac{1}{4}$ difference D	Total value of holding (A x E)

QUOTED SHARES

Type	Unit	A Number held	B Lower selling price	C Higher buying price	D Difference between buying price C and selling price B	E Value = lower selling price B + $\frac{1}{4}$ difference D	Total value of holding (A x E)

UNIT TRUSTS

Type	Unit	A Number held	B Lower selling price	C Higher buying price	D Difference between buying price C and selling price B	E Probate value = lower selling price B + $\frac{1}{4}$ difference D	Total value of holding (A x E)

NATIONAL SAVINGS

	Number	Name on account	Capital	Interest accrued at date of death	Total	Held jointly with?
Ordinary Account						
Investment Account						
Income Bonds						
Capital Bonds						
Deposit Bonds						
Premium Bonds						
Save As You Earn						
Yearly Plan						
Certificates						
(give issue number)						
Indexed-linked						
certificates						
(give issue number)						
Other						

TRUST FUNDS, LIFE INTERESTS, ETC

SAVINGS AND INVESTMENTS CHECKLIST

Enter details overleaf, filling in valuations as you complete them.

Enter details of possessions on Checklist C. For stocks, shares and unit trusts, see Checklist E.

CURRENT ACCOUNTS

Name of bank or building society	Address	Account number	Name on account	Capital	Interest accrued at date of death	Total	Held jointly with?

SAVINGS/ DEPOSIT ACCOUNTS

Name of organisation	Address	Account number	Name on Account	Capital	Interest accrued at date of death	Total	Held jointly with?

LIFE INSURANCE POLICIES AND BONDS

Name of company	Address	Name of policy	Number	Name of policy/bondholder	Amount	Held jointly with?

PENSIONS

National Insurance pension reference number

Personal or employer's pensions

Administrator	Address	Reference number	Last paid	Amount owing

DEBTS

Money owed by the deceased (hire purchase, credit, outstanding bills, bank loans etc)

Money owed to the deceased

POSSESSIONS CHECKLIST

Enter details overleaf, filling in valuations as you complete them.

Enter details of savings and investments on Checklist D.
For stocks, shares and unit trusts, see Checklist E.

HOME AND OTHER PROPERTY

Address	Freehold or leasehold?	Value	If jointly owned, with whom? And is it as 'joint tenants' or 'tenants in common'?

MORTGAGES

Lender	Address	Reference number	Amount outstanding	Is the loan covered by a life insurance policy, pension scheme or other investment?

EMPLOYERS

Name	Address	Pay number	Last paid	Amount owing

TAX OFFICE

Name and address of deceased's tax district(s)	Reference number	National Insurance number

POSSESSIONS

Item	Description	Value
Car		
Television		
Hi-fi		
Video		

Other appliances

Total value of furniture and fittings worth less than £100 (list any worth more than this separately)	

Jewellery, antiques and other valuables

Cash in hand	
TOTAL	

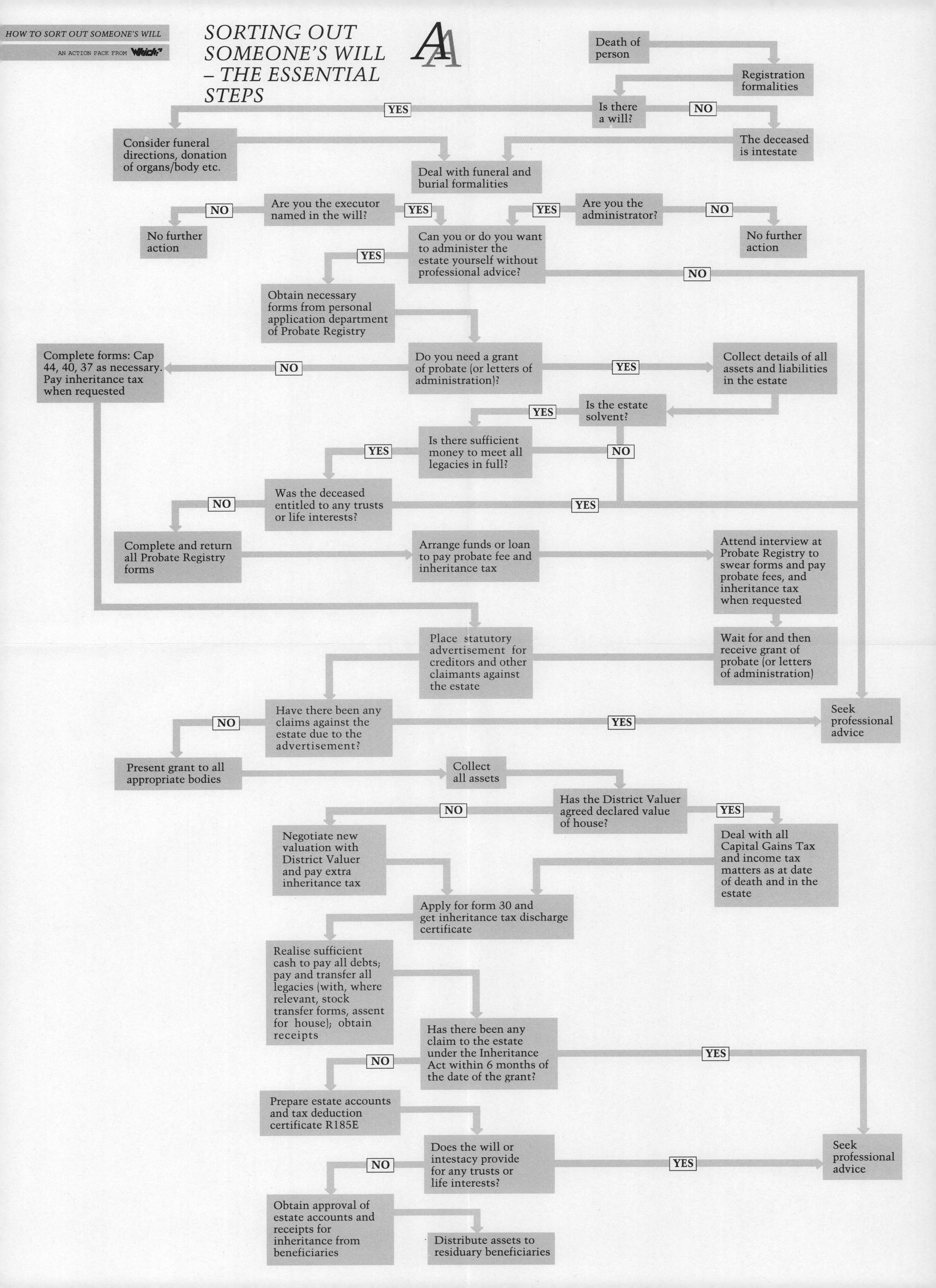
SORTING OUT SOMEONE'S WILL – THE ESSENTIAL STEPS
Death of person
Registration formalities
Is there a will?
YES
NO
Consider funeral directions, donation of organs/body etc.
The deceased is intestate
Deal with funeral and burial formalities
Are you the executor named in the will?
NO
YES
No further action
Are you the administrator?
YES
NO
No further action
Can you or do you want to administer the estate yourself without professional advice?
YES
NO
Obtain necessary forms from personal application department of Probate Registry
Do you need a grant of probate (or letters of administration)?
NO
YES
Complete forms: Cap 44, 40, 37 as necessary. Pay inheritance tax when requested
Collect details of all assets and liabilities in the estate
Is the estate solvent?
YES
NO
Is there sufficient money to meet all legacies in full?
YES
NO
Was the deceased entitled to any trusts or life interests?
NO
YES
Complete and return all Probate Registry forms
Arrange funds or loan to pay probate fee and inheritance tax
Attend interview at Probate Registry to swear forms and pay probate fees, and inheritance tax when requested
Place statutory advertisement for creditors and other claimants against the estate
Wait for and then receive grant of probate (or letters of administration)
Have there been any claims against the estate due to the advertisement?
NO
YES
Seek professional advice
Present grant to all appropriate bodies
Collect all assets
Has the District Valuer agreed declared value of house?
NO
YES
Negotiate new valuation with District Valuer and pay extra inheritance tax
Deal with all Capital Gains Tax and income tax matters as at date of death and in the estate
Apply for form 30 and get inheritance tax discharge certificate
Realise sufficient cash to pay all debts; pay and transfer all legacies (with, where relevant, stock transfer forms, assent for house); obtain receipts
Has there been any claim to the estate under the Inheritance Act within 6 months of the date of the grant?
NO
YES
Prepare estate accounts and tax deduction certificate R185E
Does the will or intestacy provide for any trusts or life interests?
NO
YES
Seek professional advice
Obtain approval of estate accounts and receipts for inheritance from beneficiaries
Distribute assets to residuary beneficiaries